BLESSED NAMES
WHY WAS HE NAMED AL-ASKARI (A)?
WRITTEN BY:
KISA KIDS PUBLICATIONS

Please recite a Sūrah al-Fātiḥah for the marḥūmīn
of the Rangwala family, the sponsors of this book.

All proceeds from the sale of this book
will be used to produce more educational resources.

Dedication

This book is dedicated to the beloved Imām of our time (ʿaj).
May Allah (swt) hasten his reappearance and help us to become his true companions.

Original Author
Abul Faḍl Hādī Manish

Acknowledgments

Prophet Muḥammad (ṣ): On the Day of Resurrection, the ink of the scholars will be weighed up against the blood of the martyrs, and the ink of the scholars will be heavier than the blood of the martyrs.
Nahj al-Faṣāḥah, Saying #3222.

True reward lies with Allah (swt), but we would like to sincerely thank Shaykh Salim Yusufali and Sisters Sabika Mithani, Liliana Villalvazo, Zahra Sabur, Kisae Nazar, Sarah Assaf, Nadia Dossani, Fatima Hussain, Naseem Rangwala, Zehra Abbas, and Rumina Hashmani. We would especially like to thank Nainava Publications for their artwork and contributions.

May Allah (swt) bless them in this world and the next.

Preface

Prophet Muḥammad (ṣ):
Nurture and raise your children in the best way. Raise them with the love of the Prophets and the Ahl al-Bayt (ʿa).

Literature is an influential form of media that often shapes the thoughts and views of an entire generation. Therefore, in order to establish an Islamic foundation for the future generations, there is a dire need for compelling Islamic literature. Over the past several years, this need has become increasingly prevalent throughout Islamic centers and schools everywhere. Due to the growing dissonance between parents, children, society, and the teachings of Islam and the Ahl al-Bayt (ʿa), this need has become even more pressing. Al-Kisa Foundation, along with its subsidiary, Kisa Kids Publications, was conceived in an effort to help bridge this gap with the guidance of ʿulamāʾ and the help of educators. We would like to make this a communal effort and platform. Therefore, we sincerely welcome constructive feedback and help in any capacity.

The goal of the *Blessed Names* series is to help children form a lasting bond with the 14 Māʾṣūmīn by learning about and connecting with their names. We hope that you and your children enjoy these books and use them as a means to achieve this goal, inshāʾAllāh. We pray to Allah to give us the strength and *tawfīq* to perform our duties and responsibilities.

With Duʿās,
Nabi R. Mir (Abidi)

About the Board ʿĀlim

Moulana Nabi R. Mir (Abidi) is a scholar, an educator, a father, and an enthusiast for creating educational infrastructure and Islamic resources for the benefit of the global community. Always wanting to think outside the box by supporting the creation of innovative materials to engage young readers to pick up Islamic books, interact with Qurʾānic games, learn from the Steps to Perfection Curriculum and begin their life long journey of holistic education.

Being a dedicated student and graduate of Darse Khārij from Ḥawzah, Moulana Abidi knows the value of Islamic education. Also, growing up in India while now residing in the United States, he has had the honor to meet with various communities and community leaders, and values the importance of collaboration and working together to optimize potentials and to create open source platforms so information and resources are available and accessible to all.

....

You, dear reader, are now part of the Al-Kisa family.
Share the word, and join the mission.

An Introduction to the Blessed Names

Our names are a very special part of us. Many times, they shape our personalities and even explain who we are or the person we would like to become. In this series, you will explore the names and titles of our beloved 14 Maʿsūmīn. Did you know that their names and titles were not just ordinary names? They were special because they were given to them by Allah!

Allah has given seven special heavenly names to our Maʿsūmīn: Muḥammad, Fāṭimah, Ḥasan, Ḥusayn, Jaʿfar, and Mūsā. Behind each of these names is a heavenly power!

In addition to their names, each of the Maʿsūmīn also had special titles by which they became famous. Their titles were often given to them because of the circumstances of their time, but these titles and characteristics were common amongst all the Maʿsūmīn. For example, Imām al-Bāqir (ʿa) was known for spreading knowledge because he was able to create many new universities and branches of knowledge during his time. However, if the other Maʿsūmīn had the same opportunity, they, too, would have spread knowledge and created universities in their teaching circles. In these stories, you will discover some of the reasons why the Maʿsūmīn received their specific names or titles.

Many of us share our names with these beloved Maʿsūmīn or know people who do. Let's learn about these blessed names and titles so we can strive to be like our blessed Maʿsūmīn!

I think al-ʿAskarī means...

_____

6

It was a hot day in the desert of Medina. The commander watched the caravan and waited until the last few people had mounted onto their camels. He then rode his horse around the caravan to make sure all the luggage was packed and safely fastened to the camels. People from all the surrounding villages gathered around to say their last tearful goodbyes.

Imām ʿAlī al-Hādī (ʿa) bid farewell to the people. They began to cry and wail as they watched the Imām (ʿa) and his family leave the city of the Prophet (ṣ). You see, the evil caliph of the time had ordered the tenth Imām (ʿa), along with his family, to move to the city of Sāmarrāʾ in Iraq. He had purposely chosen this area for the Imām (ʿa) so that he could keep a close eye on him. He was worried that he might lose his power if the Imām (ʿa) had too many supporters, so he wanted to keep him away from his followers and companions.

After a very long and tiring journey, the Imām (ʿa) and his family finally reached Sāmarrāʾ safely. Imām al-Hādī (ʿa) got down from his camel and walked towards his new home with his young son, Imām Ḥasan al-ʿAskarī (ʿa).

The home that was chosen for the Imām (ʿa) and his family was located on an army base. The area was called ʿAskar which means "army," and was surrounded by many homes of soldiers and commanders.

Imām Ḥasan al-ʿAskarī (ʿa) grew up in the area of ʿAskar. Life at the army base was difficult, especially for children. Often times, the loud noises of the horses and soldiers would startle them and keep them awake all night.

His house was like a prison. From behind the bars attached to his windows, all he would see were large soldiers with scary weapons. The children couldn't even play outside because it was so dangerous!

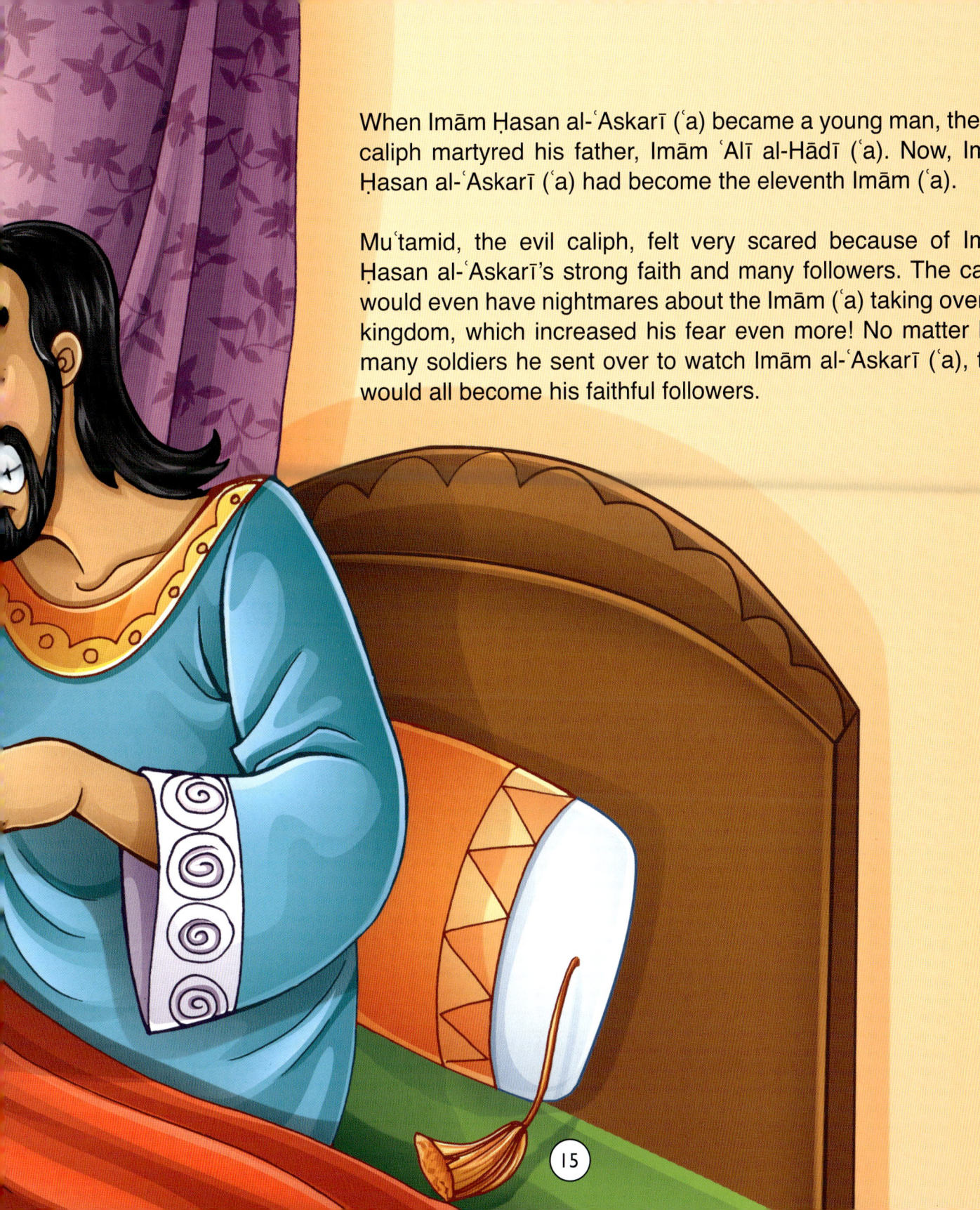

When Imām Ḥasan al-ʿAskarī (ʿa) became a young man, the evil caliph martyred his father, Imām ʿAlī al-Hādī (ʿa). Now, Imām Ḥasan al-ʿAskarī (ʿa) had become the eleventh Imām (ʿa).

Muʿtamid, the evil caliph, felt very scared because of Imām Ḥasan al-ʿAskarī's strong faith and many followers. The caliph would even have nightmares about the Imām (ʿa) taking over his kingdom, which increased his fear even more! No matter how many soldiers he sent over to watch Imām al-ʿAskarī (ʿa), they would all become his faithful followers.

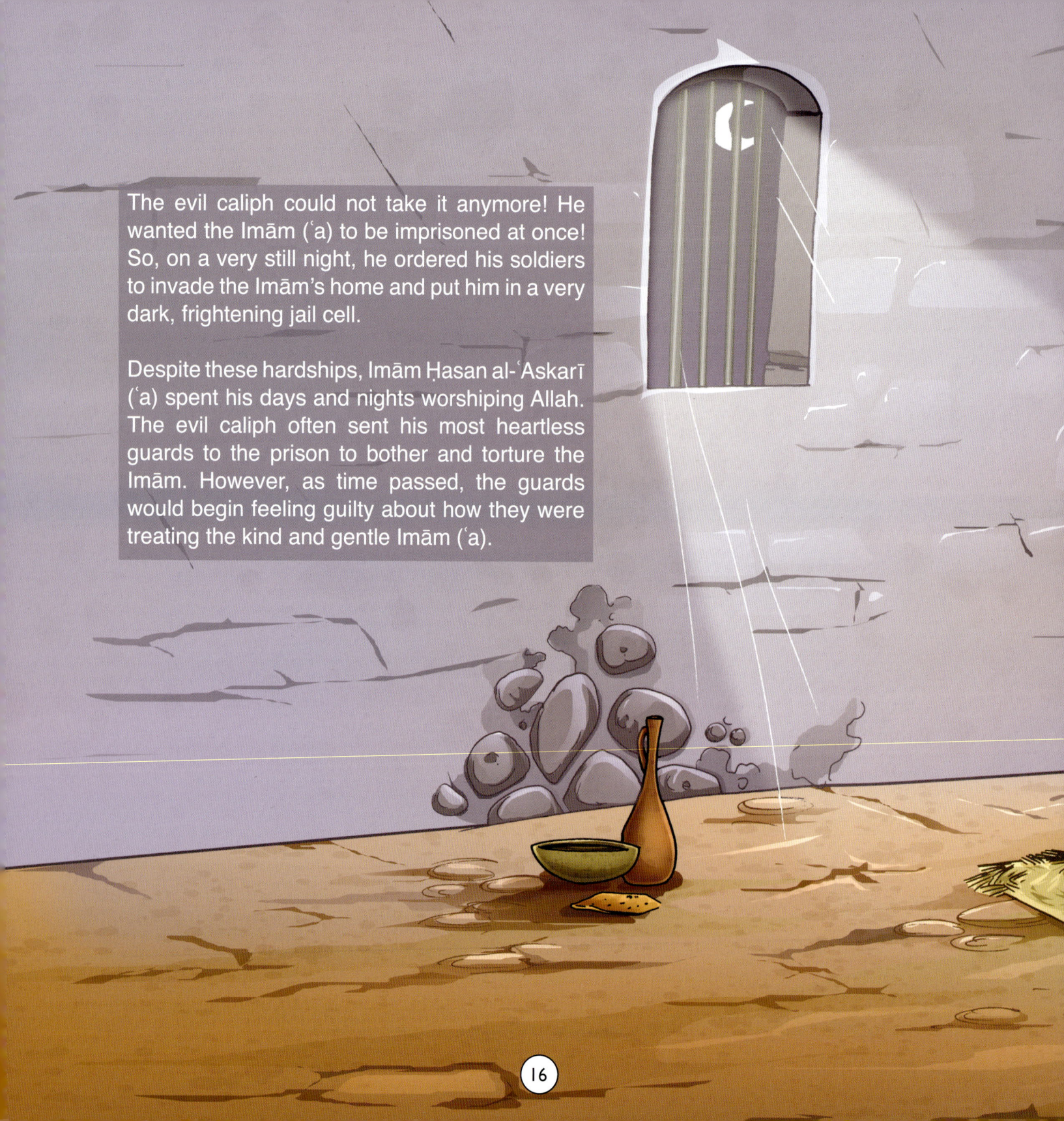

The evil caliph could not take it anymore! He wanted the Imām (ʿa) to be imprisoned at once! So, on a very still night, he ordered his soldiers to invade the Imām's home and put him in a very dark, frightening jail cell.

Despite these hardships, Imām Ḥasan al-ʿAskarī (ʿa) spent his days and nights worshiping Allah. The evil caliph often sent his most heartless guards to the prison to bother and torture the Imām. However, as time passed, the guards would begin feeling guilty about how they were treating the kind and gentle Imām (ʿa).

One day, the caliph called two guards to his palace. He asked them how the Imām (ʿa) was doing in prison. The two guards were very ashamed of what they were doing to the Imām (ʿa) and said, "What can we say about a man who fasts during the day and prays all night? He spends his entire day and night worshiping Allah. When we hear him talking to Allah, tears come to our eyes, and we are unable to harm him." Angered, the caliph ordered new soldiers to go torture and bother the Imām (ʿa).

However, anyone who would go to the prison and try to bother the Imām (ʿa) would also fall in love with him and his akhlāq and not be able to hurt him.

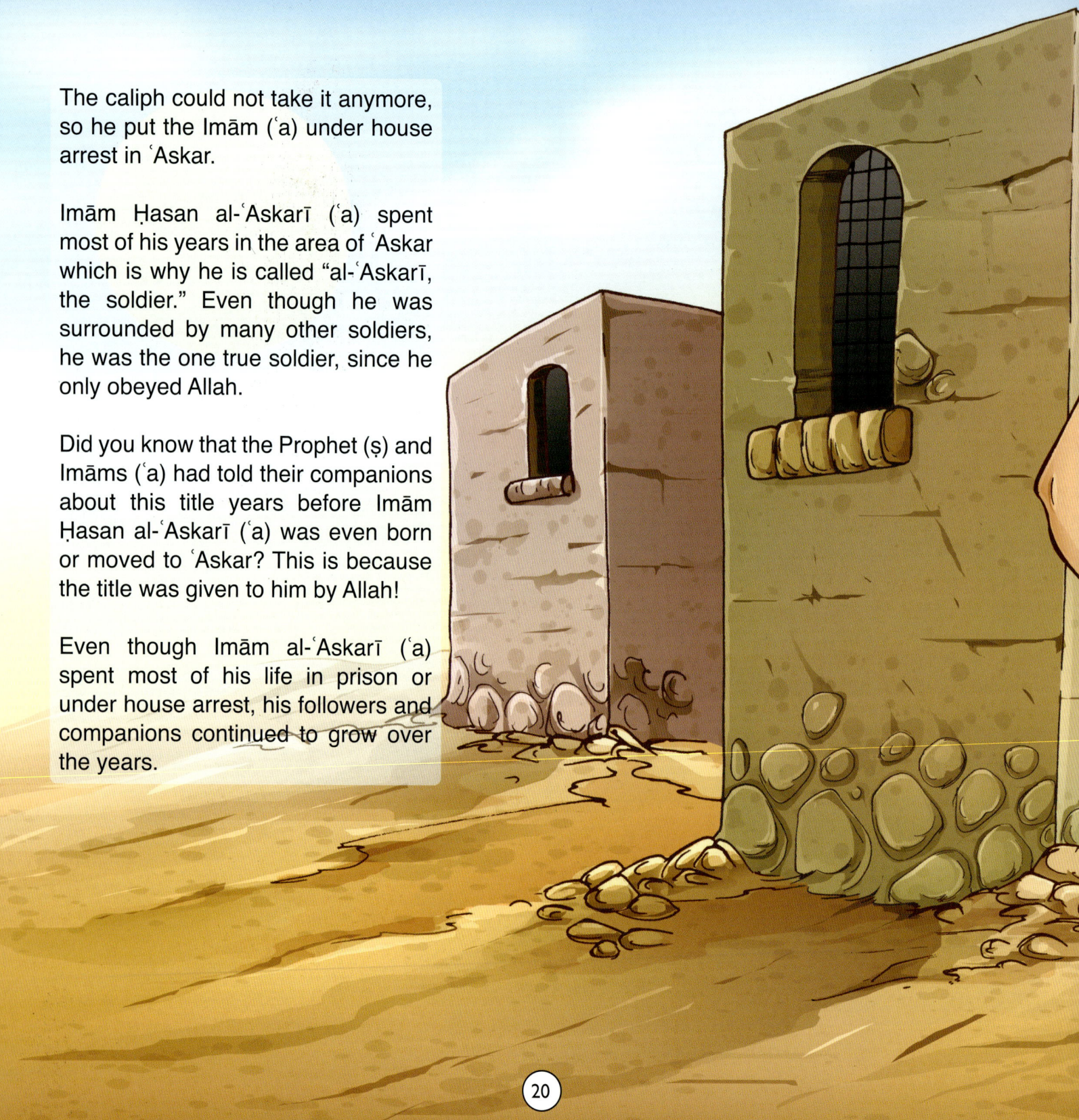

The caliph could not take it anymore, so he put the Imām ('a) under house arrest in 'Askar.

Imām Ḥasan al-'Askarī ('a) spent most of his years in the area of 'Askar which is why he is called "al-'Askarī, the soldier." Even though he was surrounded by many other soldiers, he was the one true soldier, since he only obeyed Allah.

Did you know that the Prophet (ṣ) and Imāms ('a) had told their companions about this title years before Imām Ḥasan al-'Askarī ('a) was even born or moved to 'Askar? This is because the title was given to him by Allah!

Even though Imām al-'Askarī ('a) spent most of his life in prison or under house arrest, his followers and companions continued to grow over the years.

Finally, the caliph had had enough! He realized that too many people loved the Imām (ʿa), so he decided to kill him! The caliph ordered someone to poison our beloved Imām al-ʿAskarī (ʿa), making him a *shahīd,* or martyr, at the young age of 28. The Imamate was then transferred to his five-year-old son, Imām al-Mahdī (ʿaj), the twelfth and final Imām.

May Allah send His peace and blessings upon our beloved Imām Ḥasan al-ʿAskarī (ʿa), who was a true soldier of Allah.

Ilal ash-Sharāiʿ, Vol. 1, P. 241
Kashf al-Asrār wa ʿUddat al-Abrār , Vol. 3, P. 290

Glossary

(ṣ): Peace and blessings be upon Prophet Muḥammad and his family

(swt): All glory belongs to God, the Glorified and Exalted

(ʿa): Peace and blessings be upon him/her

(ʿaj): May God hasten his reappearance

Ahl al-Bayt: Divinely appointed family members of Prophet Muḥammad (ṣ)

al-Fātiḥah: The first sūrah of the Qurʾān, which is commonly recited and sent as a gift of prayer for the deceased

Alḥamdulillāh: All praise is for God

Allah: The Arabic term for God, a culmination of all His holy names and titles

Bismillāhir Raḥmānir Raḥīm: (I begin) In the name of Allah, the All-Kind (or All-Beneficent), the All-Merciful

Duʿāʾ: Supplication; a deep connection and communication between an individual and God

Ḥadīth: A report or narration from the Prophet (ṣ) or Imāms (ʿa) that include sayings and actions.

Imām: A divinely appointed leader, sometimes refers to a spiritual leader

InshāʾAllāh: God-willing

Marḥūmīn: Someone who has passed away

Maʿṣūmīn: One who is inerrant (free of all sins, flaws, and impurities) through the divine protection and knowledge of Allah

Qurʾān: The holy book of Muslims

Salāmun ʿalaykum: Peace be upon you

Subḥanallāh: All glory and praise belongs to God

Tawfīq: Divine blessings from God (Allah) that give one the opportunity and ability to thrive towards success

ʿUlamāʾ: Scholars

Transliteration Chart

Arabic terms in this book have been transliterated according to the following guidelines*:

ء	a, i, or u (initial form)		ض	ḍ
ء	ʾ (medial or final form)		ط	ṭ
ا	a		ظ	ẓ
ب	b		ع	ʿ
ت	t		غ	gh
ث	th		ف	f
ج	j		ق	q
ح	ḥ		ك	k
خ	kh		ل	l
د	d		م	m
ذ	dh		ن	n
ر	r		ه	h
ز	z		و	w
س	s		ي	y
ش	sh			
ص	ṣ			

◌َ	a		آ / ◌َا / ◌َىٰ	ā
◌ِ	i		◌ِي	ī
◌ُ	u		◌ُو	ū
◌ّ	double letter			

*Please note that due to limitations, the transliteration is not 100% accurate in capturing tajwīd rules.